Roll of the Department Officers, Representatives and Past Commanders of the Department of Maine, Grand Army of the Republic, at the Fortieth Annual Encampment Held at Bangor June 18th and 19th, 1907

ROLL

—OF THE—

DEPARTMENT OFFICERS,

REPRESENTATIVES and PAST COMMANDERS

OF THE

Department of Maine

Grand Army of the Republic

AT THE

FORTIETH ANNUAL ENCAMPMENT

HELD AT BANGOR

JUNE 18th and 19th, 1907

COMPILED BY THOMAS G. LIBBY, A. A. G.

ROLL

—OF THE—

DEPARTMENT OFFICERS,

REPRESENTATIVES and PAST COMMANDERS

OF THE

Department of Maine

Grand Army of the Republic

AT THE

FORTIETH ANNUAL ENCAMPMENT

HELD AT BANGOR

JUNE 18th and 19th, 1907

1907
PRESS OF THE COURIER-GAZETTE
ROCKLAND, ME.

E962
.M16
40th
1907

Roll of the

FORTIETH ANNUAL ENCAMPMENT

Department of Maine, G. A. R.

Held at BANGOR,

Tuesday and Wednesday, June 18 and 19, 1907

DEPARTMENT OFFICERS

Commander, Fiederick S Walls, Lafayette Carvei Post, No. 45, Vinalhaven.

Senior Vice Commandei, Joseph J. Robeits, D. L. Weaie Post. No. 89, East Sullivan.

Junioi Vice Commandei, Daniel C Ayer, Chailes S. Bickmoie Post, No 115, Edes Falls.

Medical Diiectoi, John H. McGiegoi, Joseph Hookei Post, No 86, Lincoln, P O West Enfield

Chaplain, Rev John W. Webstei, Paiker Post, No. 151, Lovell, P O. Newpoit

---

COUNCIL OF ADMINISTRATION

John Williamson, Post No 2, Portland.
Chailes E. Moulton, Post No. 47, Auburn, P. O. Lewiston.
Samuel F Paicher, Post No. 28, Biddefoid
Robert B Cookson, Post No. 12, Bangoi.
Jonathan F. Jefferd, Post No 38, Livermoie Falls.

OFFICIAL STAFF

Assistant Adjutant General, Thomas G Libby, Post No 45, Vinalhaven.

Assistant Quartermaster General, James P. Armbrust, Post No. 45, Vinalhaven.

Inspector, Gilman P. Smith, Post No 50, Cherryfield, P O. Bangor.

Judge Advocate, Leroy T. Carleton, Post No. 21, Winthrop.

Chief Mustering Officer, Joshua W Black, Post No 30, Searsport.

Department Patriotic Instructor, Lucius C. Morse, Post No. 44, Liberty.

MILITARY STAFF

Chief of Staff, Frederick A Motley. Bosworth Post No. 2, Portland

Senior Aid-de-Camp, James L. Merrick, Post 14, Waterville

Junior Aid-de-Camp, Chandler Swift, Post 148, South Paris.

PAST DEPARTMENT COMMANDERS

*BEAL, GEO. L.	1868-69		Norway
MATTOCKS, CHAS P	1870-71		Portland
*WHITE, DANIEL	1872-73		Bangor
CONNOR, SELDEN	1874-75		Augusta
HOWARD, NELSON	1876		Lewiston
*MYRICK, JOHN D.	1877		Augusta
*HAMLIN, A. C	1878		Bangor
*SMITH, WINSOR B	1879		Portland
*BANGS, ISAAC S	1880		Waterville
HASKELL, WM. G	1881	(P O Washington, D C)	Lewiston
FARNHAM, A. B.	1882		Bangor
*SHAW, ELIJAH M	1883		Lisbon
WILLIAMS, BENJ.	1884		Rockland
*HALL, JAMES A.	1885		Damariscotta
LANE, SAM'L W	1886		Augusta
GATLEY, RICH K	1887		Portland
*BURBANK, HORACE H	1888		Saco
DREW, FRANKLIN M.	1889		Lewiston
ANDERSON, JOHN D	1890		Gray
MILLER, SAM'L L	1891		Waldoboro
DYER, ISAAC	1892		Skowhegan
CUSHING, WAINRIGHT	1893	(P O Foxcroft)	Dover
*GILMAN, J W	1894		Oakland
GREEN, WM H.	1895		Portland
CARVER, LORENZO D	1896		Rockland
CARLETON, LEROY T	1897		Winthrop
SOUTHARD, CHAS. A.	1898	(P O St Albans)	Lewiston
ROBIE, FREDERICK	1899		Gorham
SNIPE, SETH T.	1900		Bath
CLAYTON WILLIAM Z	1901		Bangor
MERRICK, JAMES L.	1902		Waterville
CHAMBERLAIN, JOSHUA L.	1903		Brunswick
MILLIKEN, EDWIN C.	1904		Portland
PERRY, HENRY O.	1905		Fort Fairfield

*Deceased

Post Commanders, Representatives, Alternates and Past Post Commanders

References. *Past Post Commander. †Past Post Commander and Department Officer. ‡Past Department Commander. ‖Department Officer. §Past Department Commander and Department Officer. ¶Past Post Commander and Delegate.

I. C. Campbell Post, No. 1, Pembroke
21 Members

Commander, *WILLIAM E. LEIGHTON

Representative,	Alternate,
J. R N. Smith	A. V. Moor

Past Commanders,

W. E. Leighton, L. G. Smith, Lommer McGlauflin, W. H. Lincoln, J C Rogers, Bernard Rogers, R. D. Campbell, R. C. Clark, A. S. Farnsworth, W. H. Wilder.

Bosworth Post No. 2, Portland
277 Members

Commander, WM. H. LORD

Representative,	Alternate,
R. N. Field	Geo. W. Richards
N S. Thrasher	David D. Hannegan
Alex Johnson	Wm. H. Wentworth
Chas. W. Skillings	Isaac F. Tucker
Wm. Waddell	Samuel Bond
Chas E. Haskell	Thos. J. O'Neil

Past Commanders,

‡Wm H Green, Ezekiel H Hanson, Harlan P Ingalls, ‡Richard K. Gatley, Wm S.Dunn,Leroy H. Tobie,‖Freder-

ick A Motley, ‖John Williamson, Arthur M. Sawyer, Chas
E. Jordan, John O. Winship, Hiram Ellis, Herbert R. Sar-
gent, ‡Edwin C. Milliken, ‡Chas P. Mattocks, Rufus
Lamson, Chas. H. Boyd, Giles O Bailey, Geo F Small,
‡Selden Connor, James M. Thompson. Frederick D. Win-
slow, Chas H. Mitchell, Albert S. Spaulding.

A. A. Dwinal Post, No. 3, Mechanic Falls

38 Members

Commander, WELLINGTON H. DWINAL

Representative,	Alternate,
George P. Merrill	Amos Tilton

Past Commanders,

Hamlin T. Bucknam, Frank R. Harmon, Geo. W.
Robbins, Hiram B. King, Isaac P. Davis, F. Edwin Dwinal,
Joseph Gould, William W. Denning, Chas. S. Tenney,
Henry J. Shackley, Norris Greenwood, Allen M.
Churchill, Tillson Waterman, Persian V. Everett.

Sedgwick Post, No. 4, Bath

83 Members

Commander, CHARLES H. MAISON

Representative,	Alternate,
Cyrus W. Longley	A. B. Crockett
James O. Burnham	Cleveland M. Oliver

Past Commanders,

James B. Wescott, Hartley K Dunton, Chas H.
Greenleaf, ‡Seth T. Snipe, George T Silsby, Charles T.
Hooper. Hugh T. Madden, Alfred D Stetson, Roswell C
Harris, William H. Watson, Sumner Brawn, Hiram A.
Huse, James R Cressey, James Jones

Gerry Post, No. 5, Monson
21 Members
Commander, *Wm H Davis

Representative,   Alternate,
Albert W Chapin   Seth W. Steward

Past Commanders,

Wm H Davis, Albert F Jackson, Charles W Morrill,
Robert T Thomas, Gustavus B Hescock, Ira P. Wing,
Charles J. House.

Heath Post, No. 6, Gardiner
81 Members
Commander, CHARLES O KNOX

Representative,   Alternate,
Geo Hasselbrock   Leonard H. Merrill
Wm. C. James   Horace Burrill

Past Commanders,

Gustavus Moore, John S Towle, M C. Wadsworth,
Chas. O Wadsworth, Joseph A Glazier, Frank B Williams,
Geo H. Harrington, James R Peacock, Augustus W
McCausland. Joseph C Morrison, James Walker, J. W P
Johnson, George W Cross, Benj. S. Smith, George W
Gardiner, Albert H Hutchinson, Dawson M. Dale, Daniel
H. Jones, Edwin E Lewis, John A. Spear, Calvin W
Smith.

Custer Post, No. 7, Lewiston
79 Members
Commander, STEPHEN H. MANNING

Representative,   Alternate,
Wm H. McCann   William Stevens
Orrington L Small   Levi Webber

Past Commanders,

Daniel Guptill, Chas. S. Crowell, Frank A. Conant,
W H Graffam, Geo. W Cappers, Hiram Robinson, Samuel
Shufelt, Alfonso B Holland, P B Merry, L C Bateman,
Roscoe Smith, ‡William G. Haskell, Geo W Babb, David P.
Field, ‡Nelson Howard, ‡Franklin M. Drew, John F Lamb,
E B. Morris, Chas J. F. Ellicott.

H F. Safford Post, No. 8, Dexter

26 Members

Commander, LEONARD TIBBETTS

Representative,   Alternate,
William C Elder   Charles W Sprague

Past Commanders,

Thomas D. Farrar, Cyrus E. Spencer, Chas. W. Farrar,
Joseph H Warren, John Nutter, T. L Webber, Stanley
Plummer, Samuel Morrill, Llewllyn Copeland, Seth Swan-
ton, Edward French.

Webster Post, No. 9, Kennebunk

28 Members

Commander, ALBERT S. BRIGGS

Representative,   Alternate,
Chas. R Littlefield   Warren Howard

Past Commanders,

William F Bowen, Enoch F. Mitchell, Almon Little_
field, Geo A Jennison, William C. Goodwin, Eli S. Water-
house, Geo F Moore.

Berry Post, No. 10, Lisbon
42 Members

Commander, *GEO R FOSTER

Representative,   Alternate,
William H. Atwood   ¶John C Steele

Past Commanders,

W H Miles, ¶John C Steele, Henry Allen, Geo. A.
Cooledge, Waldo B. Keene, Albert H Macurda, E M.
True, Geo R. Foster, Frank Foster.

Stephen Davis Post, No. 11 Pittsfield
44 Members

Commander, *ORRIN L. SOULE

Representative,   Alternate,
Henry Judkins   John Weymouth

Past Commanders,

Orrin S. Haskell, Enoch R Carr, Hannibal H Powers,
Geo. W. Patten, Richard M. Daniels, Chas Chase, Wm
L. Ross, Orrin L Soule.

B. H. Beale Post, No. 12, Bangor
164 Members

Commander, *JOHN J FLYNN

Representative,   Alternate,
Benning C. Additon   William Patterson
Warren A Jordan   Robert A. Webster
James E. Rogers   Richard H. Holeyoke

Past Commanders,

John C Honey, Henry R Cowan, Wm H Thompson,
Jeremiah S Bartlett, Flavius O Beale, Frank A Garnsey,
Fred E Sprague, Chas C Downs, Jasper I Fisher, Thomas
T. Tabor, Albert S Field, John J Flynn, ‡Wm Z. Clay-
ton, ‖Robert B Cookson, Geo E Dodge

Seth Williams Post, No. 13, Augusta
152 Members

Commander, NATHAN T FOLSOM

Representative,   Alternate,

Chas H Davis   Stephen A. Thurston
Nathaniel W White   Warren A Dolliff
Oliver P Robbins   Daniel P Hanson

Past Commanders,

Samuel J Gallagher, Arthur L Brown, Henry F.
Blanchard, ‡Samuel W Lane, Lorenzo B Hill, H A. N.
Dutton, O. O. Stetson. B. H. Swift, Lewis Selbing, Wm.
McDavid, Melville Smith, Geo F Gannett, A D. Russell,
Geo. E Gay, Albert A Nichols, Thos Clark, James A.
Jones, Oliver N Blackington, M. O. Savage, Levi M Poor,
Algernon S Bangs

W. S. Heath Post, No. 14, Waterville
47 Members

Commander, *HOMER C PROCTOR

Representative,   Alternate,

Sylvester Haynes   A Merrow

Past Commanders,

Geo. H Matthews, Anson O Libby, Nathaniel S
Emery, P S Heald, Sebastine S. Vose, Homer C Proctor,
Geo W. Reynolds, Fred D Lunt, Frank Walker, Albert E.
Ellis, Jas. H. Coombs, Geo. Phillips, John R Pollard,
Granville R. Libby, Geo. A Wilson, Silas Adams, Orrin P
Richardson, §Jas L Merrick, Chas H Nelson

Bradbury Post, No. 15, Machias
58 Members

Commander, *GEO E HANSCOM

Representative,   Alternate,

James Heffron   James L. Marston

Past Commanders,

E H Bryant, Geo H. Allen, Anson Crocker, Samuel

B. Hunter, A. M Longfellow, John T. Garnett, Asa T
McRae, F O Talbot, Geo E Hanscom

Edwin Libby Post, No 16, Rockland
125 Members
Commander, WM P HURLEY

Representative,	Alternate,
Wm H Maxey	Alden F Keizer
Geo H. Tighe	G B Thorndike
Jacob U Farrington	Lemuel S Dow

Past Commanders,

J W Crocker, ‡Benj Williams, C C Cross, John H
Thomas, Jas E Rhodes, Jona Crockett, John W. Titus,
Wm H Simmons, Geo F Thomas, Martin S Britto, J P.
Cilley, Edward A Butler, Wm O Steele, H S Hobbs, E.
M Shaw, Frank E Aylward, Wm P Cook, Henry C. Day,
Frank W Ham, ‡Lorenzo D Carver

Wilson Post, No 17, North Turner
48 Members
Commander, *CHAS. McLURE

Representative	Alternate
H. A Hersey	L C Record

Past Commanders,

James W Libby, U T Thomas A H Piatt, M K
Mabury, Shirley Merrill A P Russell, Milton Leavitt, A
D. Boothby, L P Bradford, Chas McLure

E. W. Woodman Post, No. 18, East Wilton
45 Members
Commander, *O. D LOTHROP

Representative,	Alternate,
Samuel S Carlton	Geo Mans

Past Commanders,

E H Farnum, J. L. B Farrington, Geo H Farnum,
Gustavus Pease, A B Adams, A S. Bumps, C S Delano,
Dennis Adams, O. D. Lothrop, M. L Bunker, C N Adams,
Wm H Chamberlain, John O. Hardy

Daniel White Post, No. 19, Kenduskeag
21 Members
Commander, *HENRY J HUSSEY

Representative,   Alternate,
Lewis W Smith   Constantine E Carle

Past Commanders

John H Everett, John F Dolliver, James F Beath, Wm K. Nason, Marcellus L Fisher, Greenlief Harvey, John F Ames, Hiram B Morey, Henry J Hussey

John B. Hubbard Post, No. 20
30 Members
Commander, *A C HARRINGTON

Representative,   Alternate,
John F Hutchinson   S. R Estes

Past Commanders,

Geo S Fuller, Chas A Brown, Henry D Austin, Harvey R Gatchell, Augustine K Lord, Edwin K Bacon, Darius C Nye Wm A Winter, A C Harrington.

Albert H. Frost Post, No. 21, Winthrop
28 Members
Commander, *MELVIN N FREEMAN

Representative,   Alternate
C. P Hannaford   Newall Strout

Past Commanders,

§L T Carleton, F J Davies, M N Freeman, Wm. H Pettengill, C. W Shaw, G. R. Smith, Francisco Wadsworth.

Vincent Mountfort Post, No. 22, Brunswick
66 Members

Commander, *PHILLIP R. GOODRICH

Representative,   Alternate,
Wm Mountfort   A. F Varney

Past Commanders,

Jos E Stetson L D. Howes I H Danforth, J H Lombard, J W Crawford, W C Ross P R Goodrich, H

M Doughty, A. J Alexander, J. A. Fisher, B. L. Dennison, J F. Chaney, D E Stanwood, Oren T. Despeaux, J. M. Grows, Chas H Williams, ‡Joshua L. Chamberlain

C. S. Douty Post, No. 23, Dover
73 Members
Commander, *‡WAINWRIGHT CUSHING

Representative,   Alternate,
Owen B. Williams   James A. Tiplady

Past Commanders,

Volney A. Gray, Geo G Downing, Alanson M. Warren, Hartwell E. Stowe, Wm. W Warren, Nathan C. Stowe, Gardner L Stowe, Frank A Folsom, Wm H Vaughn, Elbridge T Douglas, Stacy T. Mansfield, Chas D. Paine, Fernando G. Pratt, Edmund B. Fox, Chas M. Buck, James R Martin, Anson J Robinson, Wm W Miller, Judson Ames, Elbridge T Crockett, ‡Wainwright Cushing, Job S Bearce, Cyrus G Pratt, Danville P Oaks.

Erskine Post, No. 24, North Whitefield
29 Members
Commander, *JOHN NOYES

Representative,   Alternate,
Wm H. Douglas   Thomas Kegan

Past Commanders,

Ido Turner, F. B. Turner, John Madden, A R G. Smith, John Noyes.

John F. Appleton Post, No. 25, Farmington
93 Members
Commander TIMOTHY A STANLEY

Representative,   Alternate,
Alonzo J Odell   Silas Perham
Wm. R Smith   Harrison D Jewell

Past Commanders,

S Clifford Belcher, E S. Prescott, F. N. Harris, John M Keith, Jno H. Crowell, Dennis Smith, John E Greenleaf, Alonzo Sylvester, Levi G Brown, Isaac B Russell, Wm. D. Randall, Chas. F Coburn, Nelson Gould.

Thomas T. Rideout Post, No. 26, Bowdoinham
10 Members

Commander, *J. LOYALIST BROWNE

Representative,   Alternate,

Edward T. Jackson   ¶Chas A Jordan

Past Commanders,

Alonzo Cutler, William A. Newton, J. Loyalist Browne,
Francis I. Merryman, ¶Chas A. Jordan.

Farragut Post, No. 27, Bridgton
49 Members

Commander, CHARLES H. POTTER

Representative,   Alternate,
Samuel Knight   Wm. A Richardson

Past Commanders,

Henry A. Shorey, E M. Berry, A H. Harriman,
Daniel M Crockett, Richard T. Bailey, Wm. H. Seavey,
Frank A. Libby, Granville M. Burnell, David C Saunders,
Wm. H Foster, Geo H. Billings

Sheridan Post, No. 28, Biddeford

57 Members

Commander, *WILLIAM F. BRADBURY

Representative,   Alternate,
Eben Burnham   John W. Goodwin

Past Commanders,

John J. Traynor, Timothy Elliott, Chas. H Townsend,
James F. Tarr, Albert F Witham, Benj. P. Ross, Nahum
H. Pillsbury, George Smith, ‖Samuel F Parcher, Geo H.
Benson, John B Lowell, Jean B Pare, Jr., Chas. S Flet-
cher, Nathan W. Kendall, Wm F. Bradbury.

Abraham Lincoln Post, No. 29, Wells
22 Members

Commander, *Jno. A. Littlefield

Representative,   Alternate,
Chas A. Davis   A H. Cram

Past Commanders

Chas. H. Smith, Horace S Mills, Gideon R. Littlefield, Downing Hatch, Josiah Littlefield, Sewell L Goodwin, John L Bean, Jonathan A Littlefield.

Freeman McGilvery Post, No. 30, Searsport
35 Members

Commander, *Clifton Whittum

Representative,   Alternate,
Charles P Ferguson   Frank E Whitcomb

Past Commanders.

Geo L Merrill, ‖Joshua W. Black, Wm B Sawyer, James E Wentworth, Enoch W. Robbins, Clifton Whittum, James B. Sweetser, Elisha Hopkins, Melvin M Whittum, James A Colson. Frank A Colcord, Josiah C Dutch, Alfred E Nickerson, Alfred Stinson, Herbert T. Scribner, Leander M. Sargent, Henry M Chase, Albert S Nickerson, Jas H Kneeland.

J. S. Sampson Post, No. 31, Milo
29 Members

Commander, *Henry F Daggett

Representative,   Alternate,
Elbridge C Morrill   Palmer Lovejoy

Past Commanders.

Thomas F Hodgdon, Henry F Daggett, Abial E Leonard, Stewart D Buswell, Henry D Savage, Alfred D. Morse.

George Goodwin Post, No. 32, St. Albans
26 Members

Commander, ‡C A. SOUTHARD

Representative,	Alternate,
Joseph T Johnson	F M Wilkins

Past Commanders,

John S Parker, H. B. Allen, O. A. Parkman, A M. Bartlett, S. S Parker, W. H Lombard, Abner Brooks.

R. W. Mullen Post, No. 33, No. Vassalboro
24 Members

Commander, *ELLSBURY McCoy

Representative,	Alternate,
¶R W. Pitts	C. E. Tobey

Past Commanders,

¶R. W Pitts, S M Bragg, J W Johnson, Ellsbury McCoy.

Joel A Haycock Post, No. 34, Calais
83 Members

Commander, *JOHN A SEARS

Representative,	Alternate,
Sewall S Quimby	Michael Cassidy
Frederick W Cochrane	Andrew Keenan

Past Commanders

Henry A Balcom, Stephen D Morrell, Edwin H Vose, Frederick A Townsend, Ashley St Clair, John Larner, George F Frost, Daniel McNutt, Daniel W Sherman, John A Sears, John B Murphy

C F. Pilley Post, No. 35, Unity
17 Members

Commander, *C. M WEBSTER

Representative,   Alternate,
Chas W. Smith   Chas B Hathway

Past Commanders,
Abner W Fletcher, Samuel A. Myrick, William Hamilton, Chas M Webster, Reuel M Berry, Reuben Rhodes, Albion P Hatch, Wm. H J Moulton, Freeman Myrick, Lewis Thompson, Gideon Pomeroy, Robert W. Cook, Silas Bither, Amanda Rackliff, Charles H. Marshall

Fred S. Gurney Post, No. 36, Saco
41 Members

Commander, *EDWARD A. SAVAGE

Representative,   Alternate,
Eugene Mills   Lewis L Bean

Past Commanders,
Wm. H Atkins, Burns R Bean, Francis J. Cousins, Lorenzo D. Cousins. John Deering, Winfield S. Hasty, Wm. J. Bradford, Warren R Jordan, James B Marr, Edward A. Savage, Joseph H Shaw, Moses G Tarbox, Ernest E. M. Vinton.

G. H. Ruggles Post, No. 37, Etna
20 Members

Commander, B. C. FRIEND

Representative,   Alternate,
Noah Edminister   John Hurd

Past Commanders,
O. W. Cole. G. M. Blackden, J W. Silvester. D M Stearns. H H. Wheeler, Albert Cookson Hanson Hutchings, Stowell S Spratt J F. Partridge. Edward Friend

Kimball Post, No. 38, Livermore Falls
35 Members

Commander, *EDWIN RILEY

Representative,   Alternate,
Elias Morse   Harry Jordan

Past Commanders,

A. D Brown, C W Brown, Geo Tair, ‖J. F Jeffeids,
A B Holmes, Adelbeit Alden, Edwin Riley, C. E. Thomas,
S A. Nelke, L W Elliott, S. D. Biown.

P. Henry Tillson Post, No. 39, Thomaston
37 Members

Commander, *JOSEPH E. MEARS

Representative,   Alternate,
Rufus C. Buriows   Jas McCaiter

Past Commanders,

Nelson S Fales, Alfied C Stiout, Leroy C Leimond,
John D Morse, Olivei E Copeland, Jas H H Hewett,
Allen M. Cieamei, Elbiidge Buiton, Fiedeiick Waldo, Augustus N. Linscott, Oscai Blunt, Edwaid C Andrews, Raymond W Hoffses, Joseph E Meais

Meade Post, No. 40, Eastport
40 Members

Commander, *MORRIS CARNEY

Representative,   Alternate,
¶Walter F Biadish   No election

Past Commanders,

Geo P Andiews, ¶W. F. Biadish, Peter A Maitin,
John A Lowe, Heniy Haiiington, J H Camplin, Moiiis
Carney

Joseph E Colby Post, No 41, Rumford Falls
28 Members

Commander, *FRANKLIN MARTIN

Representative,
Chas H Tripp

Alternate,
Geo T Farrar

Past Commanders,

W. S Howe, Franklin Martin, L F Elliott, Henry M. Colby, J V Silver, Jas F Putnam, George D Bisbee, Wm Sargent, John W Buzzell.

Thomas H Marshall Post, No. 42, Belfast
69 Members

Commander, *A O STODDARD

Representative,
¶George W Boulter

Alternate,
George R Carter

Past Commanders,

A O Stoddard, T D Guptill, George T Osborne, I A Conant, Wm H Clifford, Martin C Dillworth, ¶George W Boulter, Andrew E Clark, Robert Waterman

Fessenden Post, No. 43, Buckfield
15 Members

Commander, *JAMES F PACKARD

Representative,
Isaac Fuller

Alternate,
A W Sawyer

Past Commanders,

Thos S Bridgham, David R Jack, Henry D Irish, Wm H Bridgham, A F Warren, C H Prince, Benj F Chase, H I Conant, Jas F Packard

E. H. Bradstreet Post, No. 44, Liberty
13 Members

Commander, *JAMES L KNOWLTON

Representative,   Alternate,
B C Sherman   Charles Perry

Past Commanders,

Geo. O White, J O Johnson. ‖L C Morse, W B
Morse, E P. Rowell, Jas. L. Knowlton, J R Lamson.

Lafayette Carver Post, No 45, Vinalhaven
27 Members

Commander, IRA O. ALLEN

Representative,   Alternate,
Stephen A. Colson   Stephen Mills

Past Commanders,

‖Frederick S Walls, Elisha H. Lyford, Levi W Smith,
‖Thos G. Libby, Wm. H Brown W. S Vinal Wm W.
Kittredge, Francis S. Carver, Geo S Carver, Edwin R.
Roberts. Calvin B. Vinal, ‖Jas. P. Armbrust, Jas C Calder-
wood, Thomas A. Dyer, Ivory Littlefield, Geo W. Griffith.

James A. Garfield Post, No. 46, Bluehill
62 Members

Commander. *RODNEY S. OSGOOD

Representative,   Alternate,
Herbert S. Dority   Jas H Morse

Past Commanders,

Geo W Butler, Alfred C Osgood. Stephen B. Wescott,
Sewall P. Snowman, Rodney S Osgood

Burnside Post, No 47, Auburn
163 Members

Commander, BENNETT B. FULLER

Representative,   Alternate,
Milton F Ricker   Geo. W Harradon
Geo. G. Gifford   Daniel P. Eaton
Benj. F. Beals   Albert A Young

Past Commanders,

Thos Tyrie, John E Ashe, Delance Young, Geo.
Lothrop, H. B Sawyer, Benj. J. Hill, Willard Carver, Chas.
H Cummings, Geo F. Rollins. Wm. T. Eustis, Nathan B.
Lord, W W. Abbott, Jacob T Crosby, Chas. L Metcalf,
Murray B Watson, Cyrus Hall, Wm F. Brann, Chas F.
Burr, Elias A. Lothrop, Nelson Fogg, Franklin Martin, W.
S Norcross, Wm A Miller. J. Edwin Nye, Frank F. Goss,
John N. Foster

Cutler Post, No. 48, Togus
126 Members

Commander, *WILLIAM F BURKE

Representative,   Alternate,
Frank McKenna   Daniel J Hogan
B Frank Oakes   Patrick Butler

Past Commanders,   ﹨

Patrick Hayes, Daniel McAdams, Wm F. Burke, Cyrus
A Sturdy, John J Daley, Winslow S. Oakman, Thomas
Hayes, Lewis Macord, Perley F. Hardy

Thomas A. Roberts Post, No. 49, Oxford
38 Members

Commander, JOHN W. CHADBOURNE

Representative,   Alternate,
Henry Graffam   A. Tireman Stone

Past Commanders,

C. T. Wardwell, Geo H Knight, W. R. Farris, J F.
Fuller, Cyrus Chaplin, Geo H Jones, E. P. Faunce, Anson
J Holden, Freeman B Andrews. D. M Peterson, David
Morse, Granfill Mayberry, William Martin. Chas. W San-
born.

Hiram Burnham Post, No. 50, Cherryfield
89 Members
Commander, *EDWIN R McKENZIE

Representative,   Alternate,
Frank Campbell   No election
Henry O. Moise

Past Commanders,
Henry H Bowles, V. L Coffin, Geo H Coffin, Oscar Dunbar, Samuel H Tyler, John E Haley, James E. Parker, Robert L Willey, E R McKenzie.

Asbury Caldwell Post, No. 51, Sherman Mills
19 Members
Commander, *BENJAMIN F. EMERY

Representative,   Alternate,
Ira B. Bryant   Wesley Emery

Past Commanders,
Wm Gilchrist, John W. Caldwell, F M Caldwell, C. S. Cushman, H. G. Sleeper, F. N. Elwell, Geo W. Durgin, Benj F. Emery.

J. Knowles Post, No. 52, Corinna
26 Members
Commander, *W. A COPELAND

Representative,   Alternate,
H. J. Golden   A. Mills

Past Commanders,
G. W. Hilliker, L. W. White, G R. Barker, A. P. Withee, A R Leavitt. A. Stevens, S S. Burrill J Stevens, C. Tewksbury, J L. Pease, W. A. Copeland, S R Roberts.

James E. Hall Post, No. 53, Bucksport
37 Members

Commander, *FREDERICK WOOD

Representative,   Alternate,
Norris Thomas   John Fogg

Past Commanders,

A. L. Conant, Daniel F. Davis, S. P. Lagross, Hiram
E Fogg, John Kennedy, Isaac L Richardson, W. C.
Townsend, Frederick Wood

Harry Rust Post, No. 54, Norway
45 Members

Commander, WINFIELD S. CORDWELL

Representative,   Alternate,
Wm O. Needham   Geo. A Haskell

Past Commanders,

Stephen L Ethridge, Moses E. Kimball, Wm. F. Cox,
David A. Jordan, Chas. R. Meserve, Samuel H. Legrow,
Columbus Richardson.

Wm. H. H Rice Post, No. 55, Ellsworth
65 Members

Commander, WILLIAM SMALL.

Representative,   Alternate,
No election   No election

Past Commanders,

James E. Parsons, Irving Osgood, Melvin S Smith,
Horatio N. Joy, George F. Haskell, A. W. Curtis, John F.
Whitcomb, Augustus R. Deveraux.

Larry Post, No. 57, South Windham
18 Members

Commander, *SAMUEL V. HASKELL

Representative,   Alternate,
James W. Little   Cotton M. Bradbury

Past Commanders,

Edward P. M. Bragdon, Thomas Welch, Jr., Silas B. Edwards, John A. Lord, George C. Davis, Manuel Thomas Samuel V Haskell.

Bates Post, No. 58, South Norridgewock
35 Members
Commander, ROLAND B. SAWYER

Representative,   Alternate,

J. F Woodsum   Henry Stevens

Past Commanders,

Herbert E Hale. Bradford B Wells, Steward Wing, Hannibal H Cross, Chas Longley, Albert Heald, Levi Moore, Almond Works. Plummer Butler, Eben C. Doyen.

Harlow Dunbar Post, No. 59, Newcastle
57 Members
Commander, *CHARLES E AMES

Representative,   Alternate,

Julius Jones   Thomas R. Perkins

Past Commanders,

Nathaniel B. Waters, Humphrey E. Webster, Almon Hall, Frank B. Tibbetts, Samuel L Foster, Charles E Ames

J. P. Harris Post, No. 60, North Dixmont
17 Members
Commander, *NEWELL W SMITH

Representative,   Alternate,

Horatio A. Hodge   Benj. W Hinton

Past Commanders,

Wm Harris, Chas. O Varney, Thomas B Hamilton, Charles E Parker Wm L Howes, Benj. F Simpson, Llewllyn D Smith Newell W. Smith.

Kilpatrick Post, No. 61, Fort Fairfield
34 Members

Commander, *SANBORN C MURPHY

Representative,   Alternate,
Warren C Plummer   Fernando C. Bolster

Past Commanders,

‡Henry O Perry, John L Rogers, Jacob A. Bridges, Chas E Holt, Henry C. Randall, Alexander McDougal, N H. Martin, Richard Harmon. F. M. Johnson, Geo. W. Eastman, S. C. Murphy.

Geo. E. Whitman Post, No. 62, New Gloucester
6 Members

Commander, *CHAS. N FOGG

Representative,   Alternate,
No election   No election

Past Commanders,

F. D Larrabee, John I. Sturgis, S M. Farnum, H. W. Jordan, Alfonzo Stevens, C. N. Fogg.

Geo. S. Cobb Post, No. 63, Camden
63 Members

Commander, *FRED D. ALDUS

Representative,   Alternate,
Arthur B Arey   Richard F. Pendleton

Past Commanders,

Geo F. Wentworth, Jas W. Achorn, C W. Thomas, Fred D. Aldus, Jas S. Knowlton, Thos. Smith, Daniel J Andrews, Geo. E Barnes, Geo W Ingraham, John F Clifford, Erastus T. Wilson. Frank A. Faunce, Merrill C. Richards, Wilder S. Irish, Chas. A Morse.

Geo. G. Davis Post, No. 64, Brooks
22 Members

Commander, *LORENZO JONES

Representative,   Alternate,
Francis M. Forbes   Charles A. Hustus

Past Commanders,

Albert H. Rose, John Johnson, Percia B. Clifford, Chas. M Place, Willard F Kendall, True P. Cilley, Charles E. Peabody, W. C. Rowe, Lorenzo Jones.

Wm. A. Barrows Post, No. 65, West Sumner
23 Members

Commander, *FRANK J. BROWN

Representative,   Alternate,
Sharon Robinson   James A. Barrows

Past Commanders,

Llewllyn B Heald, Geo. H Barrows, Frank J Brown, Stephen C. Heald, Edwin G. Doble, Solomon F. Stetson

Warren Post, No. 66, Winterport
16 Members

Commander, *G. H DUNTON

Representative,   Alternate,
Percival Smith   Reuben Gross

Past Commanders,

D. M. Spencer, G. H. Dunton, T. D. Eaton, Benj Atwood, Stephen Clark, Edwin J. Bowden.

A. M. Whitman Post, No. 67, Bryant's Pond
13 Members

Commander, *J L BOWKER

Representative,   Alternate,
F. L. Wyman   James Libby

Past Commanders,

Gilman A Whitman, Jas. L Bowker, Wm H Pearson, John Arkett

David Esancy Post, No 69, Appleton
17 Members
Commander, B. F. Simmons

Representative,   Alternate,
No election   No election

Past Commanders,

Wm. McLain, Joel S. Maddocks, John Lane, Benj A. Chaples, Robert S Keen. Benj. F. Simmons, L O. Newbert.

Willard Post, No 70, Springvale
30 Members
Commander, M F. Wallingford

Representative,   Alternate,
J C. Baker   Monroe Goodwin

Past Commanders

W H Rodgers, Moses Hemingway, G H. Roberts, John S Stokes, W. J. Gowen, L. H. Roberts. M. H Dorsey.

John A. Hodge Post, No. 71, Canton
18 Members
Commander, Benjamin A Swasey

Representative,   Alternate,
Benjamin F Reeder   Robert Swett

Past Commanders

Geo. W. Moore, Polaski Hodge, Ronello A. Barrows, Adelbert Delano, John P Swasey, John W Thompson, George K Johnson, Levit O Virgin. James M Shackley, Geo. F. Towle, Wm F. Mitchell, Thomas Farrow

Charles A. Warren Post, No. 73, So. Standish
40 Members

Commander, *WILLIAM D LIBBY

Representative   Alternate,
Augustus S Hutchinson   Sylvanus B Estes

Past Commanders
Orville S. Sanborn, Andrew T Sanborn, Chas H
Manson. Wm D Lilby, Samuel H Dresser. Edwin R
Wingate Leonard C Harmon. Edwin H Norton David E
Johnson. Benjamin A Dow Henry M Tarbox

Ezra M Billings Post, No. 74 Monroe
27 Members

Commander, *HENRY R DAWSON

Representative,   Alternate,
Moses Larrabee   Augustus L Clark

Past Commanders,
Henry R Dawson, Fred L Palmer, Jefferson Nealey,
Isaac F Cook, Alonzo F Batchelder, Thos R Clements,
Geo H. Fisher.

Lyman E Richardson Post, No. 75, Garland
18 Members

Commander, *SAMUEL W GOODWIN

Representative,   Alternate,
Edgar S Batchelder   Richard Champeon

Past Commanders,
Benj True, Luther M Rideout, Benson L Trundy,
Enoch B Strout, Samuel W Goodwin, Geo A Crocker.
Mark P Morton, Daniel A. Bosworth, David H Robinson.

Charles L. Stevens Post, No. 76, Castine
26 Members

Commander, *ROLAND B BROWN

Representative,   Alternate,
Chas. S Patterson   Edwin Ordway
John McLaughlin   Benj. F. Perkins

Past Commanders,

Geo A Wheeler, E. F Davis, Chas. H. Hooper, Frank
S Perkins, John I. Hibbert, Rowland B. Brown, E. S.
Perkins.

Charles D. Thompson Post, No. 77, Springfield
16 Members

Commander, *BENJ D. AVERILL

Representative,   Alternate,
Henry B Lewis   Chas F. Weick

Past Commanders,

S T Mallett, Chas H Tuck, B D. Averill, Chas R
Brown, Ira Barnes

Geo. F. Shepley Post, No 78, Gray
37 Members

Commander, GEORGE F MOODY

Representative,   Alternate,
Leonard Flint   Ambrose G. Smith

Past Commanders,

‡J. D Anderson, S B Cobb, M. C. Morrill. Jas N
Foster. J W. Mountfort. Edward L Fields, O G. Blake,
Stephen S. Welch, E. T Andrews, A P Morrill, Chas T
Mayberry, J D. Sawyer, Hollis Mountfort, L. G. Small D
W. Leavitt.

Borneman Post, No. 79, Washington
16 Members
Commander, *JAMES L. BURNS

Representative,   Alternate,
Frank E Stickney   Stephen S. Bartlett

Past Commanders,
James L Burns, John C. Morton, Alonzo Rhodes, Frank Pullen, Pearl G Ingalls, Ira R Sylvester, Jos J A. Hoffses Washington Burnheimer, Hiram T. Strout, Albion Carroll

Nahum W. Mitchell Post, No. 80, West Newfield
12 Members
Commander, JOHN P WOOD

N. A. Weston Post, No. 81, Madison
25 Members
Commander, *CHARLES C. HARTWELL
Representative,   Alternate,
Samuel Vose   Gardiner Beals
Alden Getchell   Frederick Messer

Past Commanders,
H. H. Steward, Geo. E Newell, E. H. Davis, Amasa Gregory, Chas. C. Hartwell, Benjamin B Rose, Charles C. Ellis.

Leeman Post, No. 82, Abbott Village
12 Members
Commander, ¶*JOHN W TOWNSEND
Representative,   Alternate,
¶John W. Townsend   John W Leeman

Past Commanders,
Jesse Barber, Rodney M. Warren, Lewis F. Ryan, ¶J W. Townsend. S E Evans, Hazen W. Frost·

Brown Post, No. 84, Bethel
30 Members
Commander, +A H Hutchinson

Representative,   Alternate,
Bennett Morse   J O Sanborn

Past Commanders,

A. M True, J. H Barrows. A H. Hutchinson, A S
Chapman, M R. Coburn. Ira C Jordan, H C. Barker, L
N. Bartlett. A W Grover, Enoch Foster.

Thompson Post, No. 85, Cornish
9 Members
Commander, *Edwin K Hanson

Representative,   Alternate,
David Morrill   Emerson Kimball

Past Commanders,

Edwin K Hanson, John Bradley, Oscar H Thompson,
Abner R Sanborn, Calvin E Woodbury, Nathan W. Pease.

Joseph Hooker Post, No. 86, Lincoln
29 Members
Commander, †J H McGregor

Representative,   Alternate,
Chester Nelson   A P Libby

Past Commanders

J H. McGregor, Luther Clay. Horace Wyman, Edwin
Savage, Edwin Hammond. Augustus B Clifford Horace
Graves

James E. Cushman Post, No. 87, Phillips
22 Members
Commander, *FREDERICK B. SWEETSER

Representative,   Alternate,
J. M. Teague   J. B. Noble

Past Commanders,
J M. Teague, Jonathan Cushman, Frederick B Sweetser.

Billings Post, No. 88, Clinton
14 Members
Commander, *¶JAMES THURSTON

Representative,   Alternate,
¶James Thurston   Joseph F. Rolfe

Past Commanders,
Laforest P. True, ¶James Thurston.

D. L. Weare Post, No. 89, East Sullivan
34 Members
Commander, *JOHN L PERRY

Representative,   Alternate,
Andrew Doran   W B. Thomas

Past Commanders,
‖Joseph J. Roberts, John L. Perry.

Elbridge B. Pratt Post, No 90, Fairfield
30 Members
Commander, *PRESTON M. EMERY

Representative,   Alternate,
William L. Holmes   Chas. E Choate

Past Commanders,
Preston M. Emery, Frank J Savage, Gardner A Savage, John E. Allen, James H. Holt, Albert A Nickerson, Wm Balentine, Stephen H Abbott

E. O. C. Ord Post, No. 91, North Anson
11 Members
Commander, *CEPHAS WALKER

Representative,   Alternate,
Benj. Young   Daniel Lane

Past Commanders,

D M Norton, Chas Crymble, Cephas Walker, J. W
Morin, G. W. McKenney, Jefferson Spearin, W. H. Mc-
Kenney, William H Rand.

Weld Sargent Post, No. 92 Boothbay Harbor
38 Members
Commander, *WARREN L. DOLLOFF

Representative,   Alternate,
William M Smith   Benjamin F. Blair

Past Commanders,

George B Kenniston, John H. Lake, Thomas J Emer-
son, Jason Carlisle, Martin Brewer, David H. Frizzell,
Warren L Dolloff, Rufus Auld, John K. Corey, Isaac M
Lord, William Reed.

Libby Post, No. 93, Litchfield Corner
26 Members

Commander, RUFUS S. MAXWELL

Representative,   Alternate,
Andrew J Tozier   ¶Orrin A True

Past Commanders,

Herbert M Starbird, ¶Orrin A True, G. A Bosworth,
Andrew Bubier, W F Haines, Gardiner Roberts, J E
Jack, J J Perry

Ansel G. Taylor Post, No. 95, Caribou
13 Members

Commander, *NOAH J BROWN

Representative,   Alternate,

Richard W. Withie   Jacob H Gould

Past Commanders,

Joseph A. Clark, Corydon Powers, Jeire Dempsey, Howard P Todd, John M Howes, Geo. W Wright, Noah J Brown.

Russell Post, No. 96, Skowhegan
69 Members

Commander, SAMUEL F. EMERSON

Representative,   Alternate,

Prescott Cleveland   Charles Smith

Past Commanders,

‡Isaac Dyer, Nathan Fowler, F. Marion Mills, Wm. H. Emery, S J Walton, G W. Nash, Benj. F. Bigelow, Wm. H. Weston Chas V Richards, Z. A. Withee, J. N. Merrill, Geo. B Safford, Francis H Wing, E W. Wilson, H. P. Cannon, F R Buck, Jas P. Thompson, S W Smith, Jefferson Savage.

Sergeant Wyman Post, No. 97, Oakland
57 Members

Commander, *GEO H. BRYANT

Representative,   Alternate,

Austin Bragg   Geo Hutchinson

Past Commanders,

J. M Rockwood, N P Beverage, Wm. H Stevens, Hiram Wyman, Howard W. Wells, David Pike, Cyrus W. Shepherd, John B. Hodsdon, Jackson Cayford, Everett A. Penney, Geo. T. Benson, Abram Bachelder, Geo W. Goulding, S T Thayer, Geo H Bryant, D E Parsons.

Geo. W. Randall Post, No. 98, Freeport
32 Members

Commander, OTIS L COFFIN

Representative,   Alternate,
Geo F. Estes   Valentine Wayland

Past Commanders,

John C Kendall, Edwin Rich, Joseph Townsend, Geo
A Miller, Floris E Gould, Chas. M Chase, T J Mann, L
D Huntress

Edward G. Parker Post, No. 99, Kittery
51 Members

Commander, *EDWIN A DUNCAN

Representative,   Alternate,
Joseph H. Dixon   I II. M Pray

Past Commanders,

Jethro II Swett, James W Brown, Daniel W Maiden,
Moses A Safford, Calvin L Hayes, Horatio W Trefethien,
Chas. N Holmes, Edwin A. Duncan

Cloudman Post, No. 100, Westbrook
44 Members

Commander, SAMUEL W LOVELL

Representative,   Alternate,
Albert H Larrabee   Elisha Durell

Past Commanders,

Wm II Holston, Albert H Burroughs. Geo F Hunt,
James W Morris, Woodbury K. Dana, Edward W Jones,
Chas C Graham, Roger A Foss, Eben Leighton, Geo W
Debeck, Philman Harriman, Edward Anderson, Hebron
Mayhew, Thomas J Foster, Peter S Graham, Wm. G.
Bessee, Enos Bliss, M Wm Stiles, Alphonzo Swett

John R. Adams Post, No. 101, Gorham
22 Members

Commander, *ALBERT W LINCOLN

Representative,   Alternate,
W B Hague   D. W Davis

Past Commanders,

Theodore Shackford, Stephen P Libby, Geo L Day, Walter Harding, Edward Harding, Benj F Whitney, Marshall C Sturgis, Wm Merrill, ‡Frederick Robie, A. W Lincoln, M. C Burnell

James M Parker Post, No. 105, Bar Harbor
37 Members

Commander, ASA F SMITH

Representative,   Alternate,
Richard H. Paine   Dennis Haley

Past Commanders,

D. A Higgins, E F Burns, E. C Parker, C E Southard, William Fennelly.

Jas. P Jones Post, No. 106, South China
18 Members

Commander. *DANIEL G TRUE

Representative,   Alternate,
J P Ellis   Chas Jackson

Past Commanders,

Chas. B. Stewart, Samuel C Starrett. Gustavus V Webber, Joseph H Haskell, Chas E Lowe, James S Burns, Joseph A. Banks, Alva Austen, Daniel G True

Vining Post, No. 107, Windsor
11 Members
Commander, *LUTHER B. JENNINGS

Representative,   Alternate,
¶Francisco Colburn   Frank Trask

Past Commanders,
Luther B. Jennings, ¶Francisco Colburn, Geo. E. Stickney.

W. L. Haskell Post, No. 108, Yarmouth
41 Members

Commander, *CHARLES H. JOHNSON

Representative,   Alternate,
Alonzo Quint   Thomas R. Chase

Past Commanders,
Ammi D. Seabury, Horace G Ross, Joseph A. Chase, John F. Brown, George E. Bryant, Horace P. Merrill, Charles R. Loring. James H. Doughty, Charles H. Johnson, Henry Leavitt, Lewis Nason, Herbert Soule, Geo. W. Smith.

Nathan F. Blunt Post, No. 109, Bingham
11 Members

Commander, *LYMAN G. BROWN

Representative,   Alternate,
¶Wm H. Collins   ¶Jas. B. Messer

Past Commanders,
¶Wm. H. Collins, Sylvester P. Baker, Wm. H. Nottage, Horatio B Baker, Lyman G Brown, ¶James B. Messer, S. A. Chamberlain.

Charles D. Jameson Post, No. 110, Bradford Centre

33 Members

Commander, *JAMES M. MITCHELI

Representative,   Alternate,
Stephen Fletchei   Andrew J. Chadbourne

Past Commanders,

John H. Furbish, Wm E. Bailey, Calvin H Rowe,
Joseph F Chadbourne, James M. Mitchell, Thomas McAvey

Thatcher Post, No. 111, Portland

65 Members

Commander, ALONZO P. ALLEN

Representative,   Alternate,
Thomas S Pine   Wm. W. Omsbury

Past Commanders,

Augustus H Prince, Geo. O. D. Soule, James K Mil-
lei, Lyman W. Hanson, Fied G Runnels, John C Ross,
Eliphalet Greeley, John L Williams, Daniel H. Towle.
Wm H Sargent, Sewall T. Fowlei, Henry L. Springei,
Geo. A Pennell, William Ross.

Amos J. Billings Post, No. 112, China

24 Members

Commander, *WM. PORTER PLUMMER

Representative,   .   Alternate,
Jeiemiah H Estes   Chas. A. Lincoln

Past Commanders,

James W. Brown, Freeman C. Waid, Leander B. Mitchell, John E Copeland, Lot J Randall, Byron P. Tilton,
Calvin Rollins, Llewllyn Libby, Wm P. Plummei.

Joseph W. Lincoln Post, No. 113, Sidney

16 Members

Commander, *JAMES H. BEAN

Representative,   Alternate,
Leavitt Thayer   Bernard Douty

Past Commanders,

T. S Benson, N A. Benson, A M. Sawtelle, S. C
Hastings, C. H. Bartlett, J. B. Sawtelle, Josiah Soule, S N.
Waite, G. K Hastings, J. H. Bean, M. B Reynolds

Edwin S. Rogers Post, No. 114, Patten

10 Members

Commander, *CHARLES R BROWN

Representative,   Alternate,
Horace D. Miles   Wm H. McKenney

Past Commanders,

Charles R Brown, Luther B Rogers, Charles H Gilman.

Charles S. Bickmore Post, No. 115, Edes Falls

24 Members

Commander, *JOSIAH C. MAXFIELD

Representative,   Alternate,
C. Henry Edwards   Ivory Mains

Past Commanders,

Josiah C Maxfield. ‖Daniel C. Ayer, Pascal M. Jordan,
John Mains, Stewart R. Hall, Samuel E. Tucker, Harlan P.
Tubbs, Wyatt F. Edwards

E. H B Wilson Post, No. 116, Orono

17 Members

Commander, *Chas W. Southard

| Representative, | Alternate, |
| Maitin V. B Judkins | Daniel Lovejoy |

Past Commanders,

Stephen H. Powell, Joseph McKenney, Thos. M Perry, Chas. W Southard, A. Springer McPheters, Wm H. Rowell, Frank H Oliver, Samuel Mercer, John E. Bennoch.

H. G. Libby Post, No. 118, Newport

17 Members

Commander, *W S Randleit

| Representative, | Alternate, |
| N R Witham | Alex Jenkins |

Past Commanders,

F. M. Roberts, D O. Billings, M. E Towne, Wm. S Randlett, Albert P. Smith

Eli Parkman Post, No. 119, East Corinth

26 Members

Commander, *E. K. Foster

| Representative, | Alternate, |
| ¶John B. Chandler | ¶F. B Trickey |

Past Commanders,

¶John B. Chandler, ¶F B. Trickey, Fred A. Thayer, Thos J. Peaks, Geo. B Noyes, Alphonzo Mitchell, T J. Leathers, J C Trickey, Dennis Hutchinson, J. W. Dexter, Henry W. Whittier, J. M. Ames, E K Foster, W E Jordan, C F Tibbetts

Knox Post, No. 120, Lewiston
14 Members

Commander, *CHAS. G ENGLISH

Representative,   Alternate,
Geo. W. Hartwell   Joshua G. Richardson

Past Commanders,

Danville B Stevens, F. C Tarr, Chas G. English, Wm.
Baird, D. B. Cressey, P. P. Getchell, Samuel Black.

S. J. Oakes Post, No. 121, Old Town
29 Members

Commander, WM. H. SAWYER

Representative,   Alternate,
John Carr   Wm. H. H Denmons

Past Commanders,

Wilmot P. Jordan, O E W. Hinckley, E. S. Tozier,
Geo. F Clark, Thos O'Conner, John P Woodman, Geo.
W Soper. Richard M. Woodman, Benj M. Griffin, David
Carr, James H. Jordan.

Frank G. Flagg Post, No. 122, Hampden
30 Members

Commander, *FREEMAN U WHITING

Representative,   Alternate,
Stephen Sawyer   John W. Morrill

Past Commanders,

Melville E. Walker, Everett M. Arey, Horace C Whit-
more, Melville Stevenson, E. B Maddocks, Freeman U
Whiting, Joseph S Cowan, Geo N. Holland, Edwin R.
Packard

Wade Post, No. 123, Presque Isle

31 Members

Commander, CYRUS W PENNEY

Representative,   Alternate,
Nathan Pulcifer   Elbridge Gardner

Past Commanders,

Oren L Hayden, Thomas B. Rose, Geo. F. Whidden,
James Phair, Henry B. Powers, Chas. H. Hardy, Chas. W.
Allen, Chas. C Pomroy.

Cooper Post, No. 124, Union

20 Members

Commander, *LEVI R. MORSE

Representative,   Alternate,
H Hemmingway   Edwin Hawes

Past Commanders,

Levi R Morse, H. A. Hawes, R. B. Robbins, Jesse
Drake, John F. Creighton, Geo. H Dean, L Norwood, E.
H. Walcott, Woodbury Carroll.

Robert J. Gray Post, No. 125, Blaine

17 Members

Commander, SAMUEL G. RICHARDSON

Representative,   Alternate,
James H. Shaw   Jonathan D. Snow

Past Commanders,

William C. McRaw, John F. Ketchum, S Cyrus Shaw.

Grover Post, No 126, Fryeburg
36 Members
Commander, *EDWARD J BRACKETT

Representative,   Alternate,
Wilson Webb   Joseph H. Johnson

Past Commanders,
Marcus M Smart, Tobias L. Eastman, E W Burbank, L. H Andrews, Edward J Brackett

G. K. Norris Post, No. 127, Monmouth
34 Members

Commander, *SIMON CLOUGH

Representative,   Alternate,
John A. Drugan   Freeman E Band

Past Commanders,
Edwin A. Richardson, Adelbert C. Sherman, Wm. W. Wade, Ethan Little, Jas A Cunningham, Horace C Frost, Simon Clough.

Dana B. Carter Post, No. 128, Freedom
26 Members
Commander, *MARK E. BUSHER

Representative,   Alternate,
Joseph M. Elliott   Theodore P. Thompson

Past Commanders,
Henry G. Barlow, Marshall Lawrence, Mark E. Busher, Nathan P Libby, Orlando Grant, Marcelus Whitney, Virgil D. Higgins, John Colby, John Sparrow, Frank B Nutt, Knowles Bangs, Geo W. Choate, Joseph H. Brown, Elijah Gay, Daniel Flye, Joseph P Libby.

William Morgan Post, No. 129, Athens

15 Members

Commander, *JAMES STERLING

Representative,

¶Samuel Heald

Alternate,

¶Samuel Foss

Past Commanders,

Alden Buckman, Reuben Reed, ¶Samuel Foss, Leonard B Taylor, ¶Samuel Heald, H. N Longfellow, James Sterling.

Louis O. Cowan Post, No. 131, North Berwick

8 Members

Commander, *MOSES S HURD

Representative,

Reuben Dennett

Alternate,

¶Geo S. Dutch

Past Commanders,

¶Geo S Dutch, Hiram Hayes, Charles Mescive, Reuben Dennett, Geo D Harvey, Moses S Hurd

John H. Came Post, No. 132, Buxton

19 Members

Commander, *JOSEPH F WARREN

Representative,

George Palmer

Alternate,

Milton M Ricker

Past Commanders,

Frank J Leavitt, E J. C. Owen, Elias Sanborn, J M Leavitt, Joseph F. Warren

Samuel H. Libby Post, No. 133, Limerick
14 Members

Commander, NICHOLAS PIERCE

Representative,   Alternate,
Joseph Dudley   Geo. W Church

Past Commanders,

Edwin Cobb, Lewis G. Richards, Geo. A Cove, Fred
W Libby, Wilber F. Chase, Henry E Clark, Barlow Up-
ton, Geo. H. Lanpher, John C. Hayes.

Edmund B. Clayton Post, No. 134, Strong
23 Members

Commander, *GEORGE T JACOBS

Representative,   Alternate,
Isiah Welch   Gustavus A. Page

Past Commanders,

William H. Hunter, James H. Bell, Isaac N. Stanley,
Frank Stanley, Nelson H Peterson, Oren Brackley, Stephen
D. Gates, Geo. T. Jacobs.

Charles Keizer Post, No. 135, Waldoboro
31 Members

Commander, JOHN E. RINES

Representative,   Alternate,
Barden Turner   L O FOSTER

Past Commanders,

‡Samuel L Miller, William H Levensaler, Samuel
Burrows, Ambrose Hoch, James A. Nash, Theodore S
Brown, Geo. W. Young, George C. Chute.

George F. Leppien Post, No. 136, East Stoneham

16 Members

Commander, *J J FIELDS

Representative,   Alternate,

¶Albert Littlefield   No election

Past Commanders,

Joseph W Cummings. James J Fields, Silas McKeen, Levi McAllister, Simon Grover, ¶Albert Littlefield, Henry Plummer, Burnham McKeen

John Merrill Post, No. 137, Richmond

37 Members

Commander, JAMES L. STUART

Representative,   Alternate,

Carleton Lancaster   Edwin Totman

Past Commanders,

William R. Fairclough, Warren S Voter, Cyrus Osborne, Chas R Johnson, Alonzo Adley, Chas W Price, Alvin Eastman, Isaac L Spaulding, James H Little, Asbury S Small, Chas H Jackson, Chas. E Tallman, Geo. W Johnson.

William H. Brawn Post, No. 138, Lubec

29 Members

Commander. *WILLIAM MERRIAM

Representative,   Alternate,

Thomas Fanning   Archibald Miller

Past Commanders,

Alex. B. Sumner, James B Neagle, William Merriam, John A Davis, Fred W. Morong, Alfred Small, Daniel K. Hinson.

Cyrus M. Williams Post, No. 141, Mt. Vernon
19 Members

Commander, *ALVIN BUTLER

Representative,   Alternate,
James Emery   E. L. Wells

Past Commanders,

John P. Carson, F C Foss, E M Dearborn, Alvin Butler, Geo Lord

U. S. Grant Post, No. 143, Biddeford
34 Members

Commander, GARDINER F. SMITH

Representative,   Alternate,
James F. Fogg   Edward K. Scammon

Past Commanders,

James A. Strout. Simon S Andrews, John S. Grant, Stillman H Emerson, Winborn A. Small, Amos G Goodwin, Joseph L Small, John C. Haley. Joseph T Mason, Lorenzo T. Davis. John B. Murphy, Bradbury Emerson, George R. Andrews, Franklin Hanson, Florin G Herrick.

William Payson Post, No. 144, Warren
25 Members

Commander, *WILLIAM B STICKNEY

Representative,   Alternate,
C. A Jones   C F Partridge

Past Commanders,

E. C. Stevens, Jason Spear, Alex C. Burgess. A. M. Weston, Benj Libby, Geo W. Kalloch, Lewis Hall, J W McIntyre, J R Littlehale, William F. Cunningham, Wm B Stickney, O A Spear, Emerson Creighton.

W. S. Hancock Post, No. 145, Island Falls
5 Members

Commander, *BENJ. R. WALKER

Representative,   Alternate,
No election   No election

Past Commanders,

Wm S Leavitt, Randall Gallison, Hiram H. Doble, Benj R. Walker

Fred A. Norwood Post, No. 146, Rockport
23 Members

Commander, *GEO R HEWFS

Representative,   Alternate,
William C. Snowdeal   William H. Thorndike

Past Commanders

Theodore V. Hill, Alonzo D Champney, Geo H M. Barrett, Geo R. Hewes, Brazilla H. Spear, Robert H Corey, Joseph Z. Kellar, John S. Fuller, John F. Griffin.

William K. Kimball Post, No. 148, South Paris
32 Members

Commander, *W. S. STARBIRD

Representative,   Alternate,
Lemuel Carter,   Rawson Holman

Past Commanders,

Franklin Maxim, Isaac J Monk, Geo. P. Tucker, Theron Hathaway, Grinfill Stuart, James R Tucker. Edgar T Record, Henry Maxim, Joseph Noyes, ||Chandler Swift, Winfield S. Starbird, Geo W Cole

Theodore Lincoln, Jr., Post, No. 150, Dennysville
14 Members

Commander, HIRAM FARLEY

Representative,   Alternate,
Edwin P. Bridges   James R. Cook

Past Commanders,
Edmund B. Sheehan, Geo. H. Hayward.

Parker Post, No. 151, Center Lovell
28 Members

Commander, WARREN DURGIN

Representative,   Alternate,
¶John Fox   Josiah D Hatch

Past Commanders,
‖J. W. Webster, Geo. M. Harriman, C. H. Brown, J.
C. Stearns, J. H. Stearns, J. L Parker, W. R. Kneeland,
¶John Fox, J. W. Stanford, Edwin Meserve, Benj. Russell,
E. T. Stearns, Alvin Pike, Geo. H. Moore.

Charles K. Johnson Post, No. 152, Carmel
12 Members

Commander, *REUBEN A. ROBINSON

Representative,   Alternate,
Benjamin Page   James Bickford

Past Commanders,
Geo. W. Felker, Francis L. Chase, Chas F. Kimball,
Reuben A. Robinson, Joseph P. Luce, Moses Parsons.

John A. Logan Post, No. 153, Harrison
18 Members

Commander, *WILLIAM L. GROVER

Representative,   Alternate,
Ira A. Kneeland   George Steadman

Past Commanders,

William L Grover, Alfred Libby, D B Brown, Seth
M. Keen, Eben J. Kneeland, Peter Jordan, John E. Woodsum, George M Chute.

S. W. Stratton Post, No. 155, Washburn
22 Members
Commander, *Samuel Holmes

Representative,   Alternate,
Chas. E. Dow   William Segel

Past Commanders,

Jas. A. Seamans, Wm. E Spooner, Sullivan Russell,
Moses P. Abbott, Samuel Holmes.

W. L. Parker Post, No. 156, Dedham
13 Members
Commander, *Chas. H. Dole

Representative,   Alternate,
Edward W. Moore   Amos T. Richardson

Past Commanders,

Pascal P Gilmore, Geo. F. Smart, Napoleon B Colby,
Chas. H. Dole, Alfred Condon, John A Burrill, Augustus
Blood Augustus E. Aiken.

Harvey Giles Post, No. 157, Boothbay
24 Members
Commander, *Dennis M. Hagan

Representative,   Alternate,
Austin Reed   John E Kelley

Past Commanders,

Benjamin Keller, Robert S Hysom, Pearl H. Spear,
Jas O Seavey, Dennis M Hagan

E. C. D. West Post, No. 158, Franklin
13 Members
Commander, *JOHN D. PERKINS

Representative,   Alternate,
Emery W. Smith   John F. Clark

Past Commanders,

Henry T. Whitaker, William H. Blaisdell, John D. Perkins.

Addison P. Russell Post, No. 159, Houlton
33 Members
Commander, *GEORGE H. SMITH

Representative,   Alternate,
Richard M. Rhoda   Henry N Oliver

Past Commanders,

John E. Hilton, Augustus W. Ingersoll, John Q. Adams, Henry J. Hatheway, Frank W. Pierce, Geo. H. Smith, Black Hawk Putnam, A. Harris Porter, Frank H. Ingraham, Samuel H. Powers, Chas. E. Dunn, Jas. H. Kidder, Kendall L. Jackins, Albert A. Burleigh.

Daniel A. Bean Post, No. 160, Brownfield
35 Members
Commander, GRANVILLE C. POOR

Representative,   Alternate,
William C. Rowe   Russell L. Jordan

Past Commanders,

Sidney W. Rowe. Samuel Warren, J. R. Stone, Newton Clough, Francis Poor, James N. Smith, Albert L. Hill, Jacob M. Hatch, J. W. Hubbard, Thos. Sullivan, A. W. Gray, Daniel B. Boynton.

John B. Scott Post, No. 161, Winn
17 Members

Commander, *GEORGE W YOUNG

Representative,	Alternate,
Horace Grant	Jerre Snow

Past Commanders,

, John D. Stanwood, Daniel S. Chadbourne, Joseph Clukey, Geo. W Young, Frank Leathers, Hiram P Pratt, Edward S. Davis.

William Brannen Post, No. 162, Weston
11 Members

Commander, ¶STEPHEN H FOSTER

Representative,	Alternate,
¶Stephen H. Foster	George Sabine

Past Commanders,

Josiah G Butler, Weston Brannen, Chas. L. Howard, Wm. H. Earle, ¶Stephen H. Foster.

William Reed Post, No. 164, Sanford
14 Members

Commander, PHILIP P DEHAVEN

Representative,	Alternate,
¶John M. Hayes	¶Noah W. Gerrish

Past Commanders,

Geo F. Pitts, Nathaniel C Goodwin, ¶Noah W Gerrish, Hiram W. Shepard, Josiah R Califf, Orrin F Pillsbury, ¶John M. Hayes, Jas G Perkins.

Hannibal Hamlin Post, No. 165, Bangor
73 Members
Commander, JAMES L MOUNTAINE

Representative,   Alternate,

Chas. H French   Stephen D Benson

John C Bowen   Fred C. Low

Past Commanders,

Horace C. Chapman, Chas Hamlin, Fred H Small, Henry L Mitchell, Joseph S Smith, Frank D Pullen John F Foster, John T Gilman, Allen H Drummond, Chas M. Griffin, Alfred G Curtis, Alfred Walton, George M Curtis, ‡Augustus B. Farnham, A E Fernald

William C. Hall Post, No. 166, Jefferson
22 Members
Commander, *ALDEN C BOYNTON

Representative,   Alternate,

Geo. H. Dow   Alva M Davis

Past Commanders,

W A Jackson, A. C Boynton, Hugh Kerr, A N. Linscott, A. A Skinner, James Eugley, Sylvester Vinal, C. S Noyes, George B Erskine.

Lewis H. Wing Post, No. 167, Wayne
38 Members
Commander, SAMUEL S WYMAN

Representative,   Alternate,

John R Masterman   John S Raymond

Past Commanders,

Chas. E Wing, James M. Pike, Williston Jennings, Augustus S George, George H. Lord, Henry A. Dexter, Henry T Frost, Charles M. Lovejoy, Jason Gill, John G. Daggett, L T Wing, John M. Williams Thos A Dascomb

GENERAL INFORMATION

Membership of the Fortieth Annual Encampment

Post Commanders,	150
Delegates,	168
Past Post Commanders,	1446
Department Officers,	19
Past Department Commanders,	24
	1807

Less Past Post Commanders listed as Post Commanders, Delegates, Department Officers, and Past Department Commanders,	160
Total vote of the Encampment,	1647

Number of Posts in the Department,	150
Number of Members in the Department,	5499

Representatives to be elected to the Forty-first National Encampment:

1 Delegate-at-Large.
1 Alternate at Large.
11 2 Delegates.
11 2 Alternates.

Department Officers, Delegates and Past Department Commanders present at the 40th National Encampment held at Minneapolis, August, 1906

DEPARTMENT OFFICERS

FREDERICK S WALLS, Commander.
THOMAS G. LIBBY, Assistant Adjutant General
JAMES P. ARMBRUST, Assistant Quartermaster General.

Delegates Elected by the Department

Ira C. Jordan, Delegate at Large, Post No 84, Bethel.
John F. Foster, Post No 165, Bangor.
Alex B Sumner, Post No. 138, Lubec.
A. E Nickerson, Post No 30, Searsport.
Lewis Selbing, Post No. 13, Augusta.

Elected by Council of Administration to Fill Vacancies

Calvin B. Vinal, Post No 45, Vinalhaven.
Charles Smith, Post, No. 96, Skowhegan
Warren A Jordan, Post No. 12, Bangor
Fred L. Palmer, Post No. 74, Munroe.
A H. Pratt, Post No. 17, North Turner
Orrin A. True, Pos No. 93, Litchfield.

Past Department Commanders Present

Wainwright Cushing, Foxcroft; William Z. Clayton, Bangor, James L. Merrick, Waterville.

Members on the Commander-in-Chief's Staff Present

B H Putnam Houlton; Frank Campbell, Cherryfield.

LIST OF POSTS BY COUNTIES

ANDROSCOGGIN COUNTY

Location	Post	Location	Post
Mechanic Falls,	3	Livermoie Falls,	38
Lewiston,	7	Auburn,	47
Lisbon,	10	Lewiston,	120
Noith Turnei,	17		

AROOSTOOK COUNTY

Sheiman Mills,	51	Piesque Isle,	123
Fort Faiifield,	61	Island Falls,	145
Caribou,	95	Washbuin,	155
Blaine,	125	Houlton,	159
Weston,	162		

CUMBERLAND COUNTY

Poitland,	2	Fieepoit,	98
Biunswick,	22	Westbrook,	100
Bridgton,	27	Goiham,	101
South Windham,	57	Yaimouth,	108
New Gloucester,	62	Poitland,	111
Standish,	73	Casco,	115
Giay,	78	Harrison,	153

FRANKLIN COUNTY

East Wilton,	18	Phillips,	87
Faimington,	25	Stiong,	134

HANCOCK COUNTY

Bluehill,	46	East Sullivan,	89
Bucksport,	53	Mt. Deseit,	105
Ellswoith,	55	Dedham,	156
Castine,	76	Franklin,	158

KENNEBEC COUNTY

Gardiner,	6	Litchfield,	93
Augusta,	13	South China,	106
Waterville,	14	Windsor,	107
Hallowell,	20	China,	112
Winthrop,	21	Sidney,	113
East Vassalboro,	33	Monmouth,	127
Togus,	48	Mt. Vernon,	141
Clinton,	88	Wayne,	167
Oakland,	97		

KNOX COUNTY

Rockland,	16	Washington,	79
Thomaston,	39	Union,	124
Vinalhaven,	45	Warren,	144
Camden,	63	Rockport,	146
Appleton,	69		

LINCOLN COUNTY

North Whitefield,	24	Waldoboro,	135
Newcastle,	59	Boothbay,	157
Boothbay Harbor,	92	Jefferson,	166

OXFORD COUNTY

Rumford Center,	41	Bethel,	84
Buckfield,	43	Fryeburg,	126
Oxford,	49	Stoneham,	136
Norway,	54	South Paris,	148
West Sumner,	65	Lovell Center,	151
Bryant's Pond,	67	Brownfield,	160
Canton,	71		

PENOBSCOT COUNTY

Dexter,	8	Bradford,	110
Bangor,	12	Patten,	114
Kenduskeag,	19	Orono,	116
Etna,	37	Newport,	118
Corinna.	52	East Corinth,	119
North Dixmont,	60	Oldtown,	121
Garland,	75	Hampden Corner,	122
Springfield,	77	Carmel,	152
Lincoln,	86	Winn,	161
		Bangor,	165

PISCATAQUIS COUNTY

Monson,	5	Abbott,	82
Dover,	23	Milo,	31

SAGADAHOC COUNTY

Bath,	4	Richmond,	137
Bowdoinham,	26		

SOMERSET COUNTY

Pittsfield,	11	North Anson,	91
St. Albans,	32	Skowhegan,	96
South Norridgewock,	58	Bingham,	109
Madison,	81	West Athens,	129
Fairfield,	90		

WALDO COUNTY

Searsport,	30	Brooks,	64
Unity,	35	Winterport,	66
Belfast,	42	Monroe,	74
Liberty,	44	Freedom,	128

WASHINGTON COUNTY

Pembroke,	1	Cherryfield,	50
Machias,	15	Lubec,	138
Calais,	34	Dennysville,	150
Eastport,	40		

YORK COUNTY

Kennebunk,	9	Kittery,	99
Biddeford,	28	North Berwick,	131
Wells,	29	Buxton Center,	132
Saco,	36	Limerick,	133
Springvale,	70	Biddeford,	143
West Newfield,	80	Sanford,	164
Cornish,	85		

LOCATION AND DATE
OF
ANNUAL ENCAMPMENTS, DEPT OF MAINE, G. A. R.

STATE ENCAMPMENT	PLACE OF MEETING	DATE OF MEETING		YEAR
First	Portland	January	10	1868
Second	Augusta	"	22	1869
Third	Portland	"	24	1870
Fourth	Lewiston	"	31	1871
Fifth	Biddeford	"		1872
Sixth	Bangor	"	29	1873
Seventh	Augusta	"	29	1874
Eighth	Skowhegan	"	28	1875
Ninth	Auburn	"	21	1876
Tenth	Gardiner	"	23	1877
Eleventh	Biddeford	"	23	1878
Twelfth	Bangor	"		1879
Thirteenth	Lewiston	"	29	1880
Fourteenth	Rockland	February	22	1881
Fifteenth	Gardiner	"	8	1882
Sixteenth	Auburn	"	6	1883
Seventeenth	Waterville	"	20	1884
Eighteenth	Thomaston	"	18	1885
Nineteenth	Skowhegan	"	10	1886
Twentieth	Bath	January	25	1887
Twenty-first	Portland	February	9	1888
Twenty-second	Lewiston	"	7	1889
Twenty-third	Augusta	"	3	1890
Twenty-fourth	Portland	"	18	1891
Twenty-fifth	Auburn	"	4	1892
Twenty-sixth	Rockland	"	9	1893
Twenty-seventh	Bangor	"	6	1894
Twenty-eighth	Skowhegan	"	12	1895
Twenty-ninth	Bangor	"	18	1896
Thirtieth	Lewiston	April	15	1897
Thirty-first	Waterville	February	24	1898
Thirty-second	Bangor	"	16	1899
Thirty-third	Portland	"	14	1900
Thirty-fourth	Auburn	"	19	1901
Thirty-fifth	Augusta	"	13	1902
Thirty-sixth	Bangor	"	18	1903
Thirty-seventh	Bangor	"	17	1904
Thirty-eighth	Lewiston	"	16	1905
Thirty-ninth	Portland	June	13	1906
Fortieth	Bangor	"	18	1907

DEPARTMENTS

IN ORDER OF SENIORITY ACCORDING TO DATE
OF PERMANENT ORGANIZATION

1	Illinois	July 12, 1866
2	Wisconsin	September, 1866
3.	Pennsylvania	January 16, 1867
4	Ohio	January 30, 1867
5	New York	April 3, 1867
6	Connecticut	April 11, 1867
7	Massachusetts	May 7, 1867
8	New Jersey	December 10, 1868
9	Maine	January 10, 1868
10	California and Nevada	February 21 1868
11	Rhode Island	March 24 1868
12	New Hampshire	July 30, 1868
13	Vermont	October, 23, 1868
14	Potomac	February 13, 1869
15	Virginia and North Carolina	July 27, 1871
16	Maryland (re-organized)	June 9, 1876
17	Nebraska (re-organized)	June 11, 1877
18	Michigan (re-organized	January 6, 1879
19	Iowa (re-organized)	January 23, 1879
20	Indiana (re-organized)	October 3, 1879
21	Colorado and Wyoming	December 11, 1879
22	Kansas (re-organized)	March 16 1880
23	Delaware (re-organized)	January 14 1881
24	Minnesota (re-organized)	August 17, 1881
25	Missouri (re-organized)	April 22, 1882
26	Oregon (re-organized)	September 28 1882
27	Kentucky (re-organized)	January 17 1883
28	West Virginia (re-organized)	February 20, 1883
29	South Dakota	February 20, 1883
30	Washington and Alaska (re-organized)	June 20, 1883
31	Arkansas	July 11, 1883
32	New Mexico (re-organized)	July 14, 1883
33	Utah	October 8, 1883
34	Tennessee	February 26, 1884
35	Louisiana and Mississippi	May 15, 1884
36	Florida	June 19, 1884
37	Montana	March 10, 1885
38	Texas	March 25, 1885
39	Idaho	January 11, 1888
40	Arizona	January 17 1888
41	Georgia	January 25, 1889
42	Alabama	March 12, 1890
43	North Dakota	April 23, 1890
44	Oklahoma	August 7, 1890
45	Indian Territory	July 3, 1891

Lightning Source UK Ltd.
Milton Keynes UK
UKHW011301031220
374527UK00003B/412